The Story of Science

The Miracle of Immunity

by William L. Donnellan

BENCHMARK BOOKS

MARSHALL CAVENDISH
NEW YORK

Series Editor: Roy A. Gallant

Series Consultants:

LIFE SCIENCES
Dr. Edward J. Kormondy
Chancellor and Professor of Biology (retired)
University of Hawaii-Hilo/West Oahu

PHYSICAL SCIENCES
Dr. Jerry LaSala
Department of Physics
University of Southern Maine

Benchmark Books
Marshall Cavendish
99 White Plains Road
Tarrytown, NY 10591-9001

Library of Congress Cataloging-in-Publication Data
Donnellan, William Lorne, 1925-
  The miracle of immunity / by William L. Donnellan.
    p. cm. — (The story of science)
Includes bibliographical references and index.
Summary: Chronicles discoveries made since ancient times in learning
about disease and how the body's immune system fights and conquers it.
  ISBN 0-7614-1425-8
  1. Immune system—Juvenile literature. 2. Immune
system—History—Juvenile literature. [1. Immune system. 2. Immune system—History.] I. Title.
II. Series.
  QR181.8 .D665 2002
  616.07'9—dc21

                          2001005939

Photo research by Linda Sykes Picture Research, Hilton Head, SC
Diagrams by Ian Worpole on pp. 12, 26, 43, 46, 52, 54, 56, 62, and 67

Cover: Ships in the Middle Ages and Renaissance were kept in quarantine, not being allowed to land at ports for forty days after their arrival in order to prevent spreading disease. The original meaning of the word quarantine was "forty days."

The Granger Collection: Cover, 8, 13, 14, 15, 17, 21, 22, 23 top, 25, 30, 31 (right), 33, 36, 37 (bottom), 39; Gelderblom/Eye of Science/SPL/Photo Researchers: 1; British Museum, London/SEF/Art Resource NY: 7; Louvre, Paris/Erich Lessing/Art Resource NY: 9 (bottom), 10; Christine Osborne/Corbis: 9 (top); Hulton/Getty Images: 11, 19, 41; Stephen Dalton/Photo Researchers: 18; Roy A. Gallant: 20; AKG London: 23 (bottom); Paul Almasy/Corbis: 28; I. Rantala/ Photo Researchers: 31 (left); Custom Medical Stock: 34, 35; Corbis: 37 (top); Biophoto Associates/Photo Researchers: 43 (top left); J. Berger/Photo Researchers: 43 (top right); Norbert Wu/Peter Arnold: 44; Manfred Kage/Peter Arnold: 49; Prof. P. Motta/Dept. of Anatomy/University La Sapienza, Rome/Photo Researchers: 51; Andrew Syred/Science Photo Library/Photo Researchers: 53; Prof. S. H. E. Kaufmann and Dr. J. R. Golecki/Science Photo Library/Photo Researchers: 58; Photo Researchers: 61; Shinichi Nurata/PPS/Photo Researchers: 65.

Cover design by Bob O'Brien

Printed in Hong Kong
6 5 4 3 2 1

For Laura

My wife, companion, friend

No one need be surprised that the subject of contagion was not clear to our ancestors.

—*Heironymus Fracastorius*

from On Contagion, *Verona, 1546*

Contents

One
Disease, Gods, and Witch Doctors   6
Deities and Doctors • Hippocrates and
Scientific Medicine • Birth of the Four Humors
• Symptoms and Crises

Two
Rat Fleas, Plagues, and Microscopes   16
Rat Fleas and Epidemics • Some People Are Immune,
Others Are Not • Germs and Microscopes

Three
Germs, Diseases, and Cells   24
The Germ Theory of Disease • Controlling Disease
Germs • Cows and Vaccines • The Discovery of
Living Cells

Four
Wine, Hens, and Phagocytes   32
Pasteur, the Miracle Worker • Success and Tragedy
• From Bacteria to Bacteriology

Five
The Innate Immune System   40
Natural Immunity and How It Began
• How Macrophages Do Their Work • The
Complement Immune System

Six
The Acquired Immune System
50

Two Types of Lymphocytes • How the Body
Fights Infection • Does the Immune System Ever Fail?

Seven
Immunity Today
60

Effects of Vaccinations • AIDS • Antibiotics and
Their Abuse • What's in the Future?

Glossary
70

Diseases Mentioned in This Book
73

Further Reading
76

Index
77

One

Disease, Gods, and Witch Doctors

Malaise is a fancy word that means "feeling bad." Sick or injured animals lie quietly until they begin to feel better. Humans do this too, but we also try to understand what causes our illnesses. The ideas about disease and illness in ancient times were very different from ours today.

Deities and Doctors

People looked at disease differently five thousand years ago. The ancient Egyptians had many physicians, including specialists such

Ramses III, Pharaoh of Egypt in the 20th Dynasty, 1198–1167 B.C., in the presence of two important gods. The pharaohs were the chief physicians as well as the rulers of the kingdom, and they were worshiped as gods after they died.

as eye doctors and those treating the stomach. Some of the work of these physicians was highly advanced, but both priests and physicians relied heavily on superstition, as had the Stone Age peoples before them.

Among the first caregivers were people called shamans. They helped the injured, attended mothers during childbirth, and treated sick children. Modern-day shamans in many parts of the world know a great deal about plant medicines. The Bushmen of South Africa recognize more than eighty different types of medicinal plants. Medicine men also perform chants and rituals to influence their gods. Some are individuals claiming great authority who maintain their power by using poisonous drugs and fearful threats in their communities. They are called witch doctors.

As ancient populations grew larger, their tribal leaders became recognized as kings or emperors, and the medicine men became priests. These authorities often used myths and far-fetched

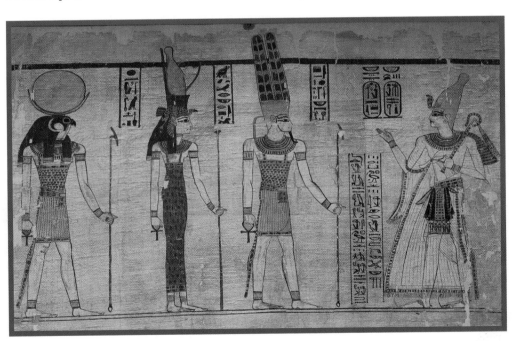

explanations for life's problems. In ancient times myths were usually related to the powers of the Sun, Moon, stars, and planets, which were all thought to direct human affairs and were given the names of gods. Certain gods were thought to protect people's health. One such god was Asclepius, the Greek god of medicine and healing. The Babylonian goddess Ishtar and the Greek goddess Hygeia took particular interest in diseases of women and children.

Some thirty-five hundred years ago in Babylon, most people believed that illness and disease were due to evil spirits magically entering a person's body. A witch doctor or priest visiting a sick person's home would look around for good or bad signs. If he saw a

Medicine men and shamans mix and administer herbal medicines. Sometimes, they perform healing dances during which they go into a trance to "absorb" illnesses into their own bodies.

This African witch doctor, dressed in full regalia, is flanked by drummers and other musicians who make his performance seem even more dramatic.

black dog or a black pig near the house, this was an omen that the person would die. A white pig meant the person would get well. If the sick person ground his or her teeth, and if the hands and feet shook, it was said to be the work of the Moon god, Sin, and the person would die.

Although some caregivers performed operations, they had little understanding of how the body worked. For example, they looked on the heart as the center of creative intelligence rather than a strong, muscular pump that sends blood throughout the body. They could have learned about the body by comparing diseased organs of people who died of illnesses with healthy organs from people killed in battle. But this was not allowed by religious beliefs of the time. In treating the sick the priestly physicians were fairly safe, but to be a surgeon could be risky. The law read that if a surgeon performed an operation and the patient died or was blinded, the surgeon's hand would be cut off, or he might even be killed if the patient was a high official.

Hammurabi, a king of Babylon (1792–1750 B.C.), explains the laws of his kingdom to the seated Sun god, Shamash. Many of the laws concerned medical and surgical matters. They were engraved on a black marble column one hundred feet high.

In the different civilizations that developed throughout the Middle East, Egypt, Greece, and Rome, the number of recognized gods increased over the ages, eventually totaling more than five hundred. While the physicians of the time tried to treat patients with herbs and by other means, they and the witch doctors also relied on superstitious beliefs and appealed to their gods to drive away an illness. Eating the heart of a lion or of a brave human enemy was supposed to make a person courageous. Eating the fat of a hairy animal, such as a bear, was thought to cure baldness. Snake oil rubbed into the skin of an athlete might improve his performance. Diseased children in Egypt were made to swallow a skinned mouse in the belief that it might cure the illness.

Hippocrates and Scientific Medicine

It wasn't until around 500 B.C. in Greece that physicians began to search in earnest for the true nature of illnesses. This marked the beginning of *rational* medicine as opposed to superstition. At that time, many different theories purported to explain the "evils" that could attack the human body.

Sculpture of the famous Greek physician Hippocrates, who lived from 460 to 377 B.C.

The most important among this new breed of healers was the Greek physician Hippocrates, who started scientific medicine. He was born around 460 B.C. on the Greek island of Cos. Since his father was a prominent physician at the healing temple of Cos, Hippocrates received an excellent education at its medical school. After several years at home he studied medicine in Egypt, Greece, Sicily, and in many parts of the Middle and Far East. By then he had absorbed all the medical and

A doctor of ancient Greece examines the chest of a young patient, around 350 B.C.

surgical knowledge of his time. Today we know of fifty-nine books that he and his associates wrote on different medical subjects. They include works on ancient medicine, epidemics, medical law, surgery, and the use of all the plant and chemical medicines known at that time.

Hippocrates was the first to emphasize that diseases happen naturally and are not acts of the spirit world. In his writings about the disease epilepsy, then called "the sacred disease," Hippocrates denied that *any* disease could be caused by spirits or gods. He insisted that "this notion of epilepsy's divinity is kept up by our inability to comprehend the disease." The writings of Hippocrates also presented an important theory that was to rule medicine for many centuries: his doctrine of the humors.

Birth of the Four Humors

Hippocrates believed that good health depends on a normal balance of different fluids in the body. This was not a new idea. It came from an earlier belief that all things in the world are built up from four root substances the old Greeks called "elements." The elements were earth, air, fire, and water. However, they were not anything like the true chemical elements we know today. The nature of the four elements was explained by the philosopher Empedocles, who lived in Sicily from 494 B.C. to

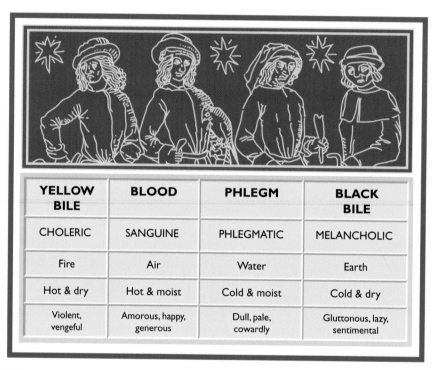

YELLOW BILE	BLOOD	PHLEGM	BLACK BILE
CHOLERIC	SANGUINE	PHLEGMATIC	MELANCHOLIC
Fire	Air	Water	Earth
Hot & dry	Hot & moist	Cold & moist	Cold & dry
Violent, vengeful	Amorous, happy, generous	Dull, pale, cowardly	Gluttonous, lazy, sentimental

Physicians of ancient Greece believed that good health and a person's personality and character were linked with the four humors of yellow bile, blood, phlegm, and black bile. They also supposed that the humors were associated with the four root elements—fire, air, water, and earth. The four qualities of matter—hot, dry, moist, and cold—combined in various ways and also were associated with the four humors and root elements.

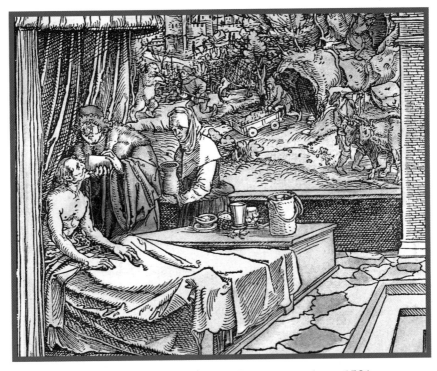

A medieval physician administering medicines around A.D. *1531.*

430 B.C. Empedocles was also a mathematician, physician, and engineer. When he was asked to clear up a severe epidemic of fever in Sicily, he did so by draining wet marshes around the city. Since mosquitoes that grew in swamps happened to carry the malaria germs that caused the disease, the epidemic was stopped, although Empedocles did not know why.

Empedocles was proud of his successes. He was also a boastful man who believed he was equal to the gods. When he was old and very successful, he announced to one and all: "I am an immortal god unto you. Look on me no more as a mortal." He is said to have written six thousand verses on medicine alone, and his theories about life and the composition of living things became very popular.

The elements of Empedocles were supposed to combine in certain ways to produce four qualities—cold, hot, dry, and wet. Guided by Empedocles's thinking, Hippocrates said that there must also be four main body fluid humors somehow associated with the four qualities. Those humors were phlegm, which we sometimes cough up when we have a cold; blood released through a cut; yellow bile found during vomiting; and black bile, which was often passed from the stomach and intestines during severe illnesses.

Physicians who followed the teachings of Hippocrates tried to keep the four humors in "good balance." Doing so required attention to a number of things, such as diet, rest, and taking various medicines. Patients were also "bled" because it

A medieval surgeon amputates a leg. The assistant is holding an anesthetic sponge that might have helped to ease the pain when its contents were inhaled.

was believed the process got rid of their bodily poisons. Good doctors relied on the body's natural healing powers, but they really had no idea how good health was maintained. They carefully watched their sick patients and were quick to change an unsuccessful treatment. Whenever patients did get better, physicians took credit for their cures; when their patients didn't improve, they blamed the gods or evil forces.

Symptoms and Crises

Fevers, weakness, and headaches are the usual signs, or *symptoms*, of sickness. Doctors of ancient times usually treated disease symptoms only, because they had no way of knowing the real cause of the disease. One important idea in medicine was the "crisis." A crisis was a sudden change in the patient's condition. It might be a good change, or it might signal a failing condition. Those ideas—as simple as they may sound—formed the basis of medical treatment until well into the 1800s, more than two thousand years after Hippocrates's time. We now know that such crises are caused in large part by the body's natural methods of fighting disease.

The story of how we learned about disease and how the body fights it is a long one. It involves hundreds of discoveries by physicians, chemists, biologists, and other scientists. In the chapters that follow we will talk about some of those discoveries. Along the way we will find out about a number of disease agents and how they work. All the while our focus will be on the body as a marvelous chemical machine that protects us from disease, even without the help of physicians or the invisible hand of the spirits and gods of old. This marvel of human chemistry and biology is called the *immune system*. It is a fantastic world of different kinds of body cells all working together to keep a person healthy. This system has been developed by nature ever since life began and is one of its greatest works of art.

Phillipus Bombastus Aurelius Paracelsus (1493–1541) searched for chemical mixtures that would cure all diseases. Because he did not believe in the humoral theory, he was not popular with his colleagues.

Two

Rat Fleas, Plagues, and Microscopes

In the 1300s a dreaded disease called the Black Death swept over Europe and parts of Asia, killing about three quarters of the population. Imagine a city of one hundred thousand people in which seventy-five thousand have died within a few weeks. The sickness, called the *plague*, came suddenly, causing violent headaches and inflamed eyes. The throat and tongue began to bleed, a choking cough tortured the throat and chest, and the skin swelled and blackened. People everywhere fell to their knees in the street and prayed to be spared the awful sickness. But soon—sometimes after only a few hours—many victims were dead.

The Black Death, or plague, killed thousands of people in London during 1665. Most were buried in mass graves. The next year, most of London burned in a great fire, and the plague disappeared.

Whenever the plague struck, people who could afford to do so moved out of the crowded cities and into the countryside. Where there were fewer people, there seemed to be a better chance to avoid the disease.

Rat Fleas and Epidemics

No one knew what caused the plague or how it was spread. Today we know that rat fleas carry the plague germs that cause the Black Death. The fleas were passed from rat to rat, each rat then becoming sick. As the rats died, their fleas deserted them and went on to bite people.

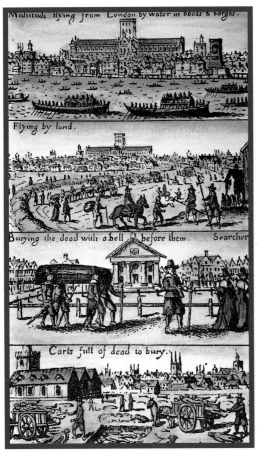

Around 1348, people nearly everywhere in Europe began to get the disease. During the next five years more than 30 million people died of it. Similar outbreaks occurred over the next four hundred years, and the plague eventually killed more than 50 million in a European population that had only a little more than 100 million people.

The plague was spread throughout Europe by trading ships, all of which were infested with rats. When a ship docked in a port, the rats scurried down the ropes holding the ship to the dock and ran free through the town, where their fleas infected people. While some people did not get sick, most did catch the disease and more than half of them died. Those who were sick coughed out billions of plague germs, which quickly spread and infected more people. The dying and dead piled up in the city streets because they could not be attended to or buried fast enough.

Rats carrying plague ran down ships' ropes onto the docks. They then spread plague into port cities, from which it further spread into many other communities.

The ancient Greek historian Thucydides wrote about another great plague that wiped out half the population of Athens way back in 431 B.C. It started in southern Egypt, moved westward to Libya, and then crossed the Mediterranean Sea to land in the port city of Piraeus near Athens. It was probably smallpox, a disease that was not the same as the Black Death, but just as deadly.

More recently, in the spring of 1918, an outbreak of influenza, or flu, caused people to complain of fever, sore throat, and coughing. During that summer, more and more cases were reported. Late in the year millions of people in various parts of the world became ill, and many were dying. During the next ten months, the flu killed at least 550,000 people in the United States. In India 20 million died, and by the spring of 1919 more than 30 million people had perished around the world. Even in places that had very little contact with modern civilization, such as Western Samoa, people were made ill by this flu. One-third of Samoa's population—38,000 people—died in the 1918–1919 epidemic.

Tent cities were set up to treat patients during the influenza epidemic of 1918–1919. These open-air hospitals were better than enclosed treatment centers at preventing the spread of disease. Masks were worn by all.

Leprosy was a widely known and feared disease that spread slowly from one person to another. Called lepers, people with the disease broke out with ugly sores, and they lost fingers and toes. So fearful were people of catching the disease that lepers were made to wear rattles to warn of their presence as they walked through the streets. Their discarded clothes were burned. Strangely, some people never came down with leprosy, plague, or the flu. No one understood why.

Some People Are Immune, Others Are Not

One thing that puzzled doctors in ancient times was why some people became sick with plague or other epidemic disease but others did not. Diseases seemed to spread most easily in cities, where people lived closely together. Without a sound theory about germs it was impossible to know how one person transmitted a disease to others. So the best thing to do was avoid other people.

Thucydides had written that those who remained well during an epidemic must have some kind of natural defense. Those who caught the disease but survived, he wrote, seemed not to catch it again. Here was an early observation of what we now call the immune defenses. But at the time of Thucydides, and for the next two thousand years, the idea of an immune system was impossible to grasp because no one knew anything about germs. This was partly because no one knew about the complicated chemistry of the human body. Without such knowledge it was not possible to treat diseases scientifically. All that the doctors could do was try this or that treatment and hope that it worked. Many of their cures were medicines made from plants.

Leprosy is still a problem in Africa. This man has lost his fingers and toes to the disease.

One Roman medical officer named Dioscorides, around the year A.D. 60, described more than five hundred plant remedies. His book was used in Europe for many centuries as a guide to medical treatment. The use of plants for treating diseases dates far back to the time when witch doctors and other healers believed that trees and other plants were the homes of spirits. At one time or another the juices of virtually every known plant have been used to treat disease. Although most did no good at all, some herbal treatments proved beneficial. Many of these are widely used by drug makers today. The Chinese developed many herbal medicines, including one called ephedrine that we still use as a remedy for colds.

Some plant medicines were found to be fatally poisonous and were often used in the practice of black magic. In the Middle Ages the making of such poisonous brews was considered a fine art. Many schemers, such as the Italian Borgia family, used some of these drugs to murder their competitors.

Germs and Microscopes

Until the time of reasonably good microscopes, little could be learned about germs. Ancient peoples believed that the gods caused disease. Later some thought, and correctly so, that tiny invisible creatures might cause illness. Around 60 B.C., the Roman writer Varro said that "in swampy places small animals live that cannot be discerned with the eye, and they…cause serious illnesses." Doctors of the time had seen enough wounds to know that the signs of infection were redness, swelling, heat, and pain, so they suspected that something must get in to cause those symptoms. They also knew that the best cure for an infected cut was to clean the wound with water and wine

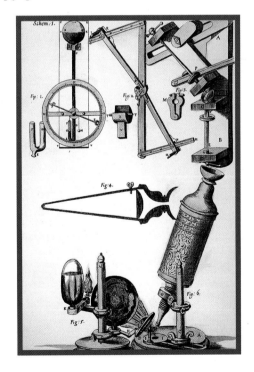

Microscopes were invented around A.D. 1600. They were beautiful, and had two lenses, but could magnify an image only by twenty to thirty times its actual size. They were lit by candles or oil lamps. This microscope, dating to the mid-1600s, belonged to Robert Hooke.

and then keep it open until it healed. But without any chemical understanding or microscopes to see germs at work, no further progress could be made.

In 1665 the English scientist Robert Hooke wrote a book called *Micrographia*. In it he described all sorts of interesting things not visible to the eye alone. Among them were the tiny openings left in wood when the living parts of the tree died. To Hooke they looked like the cells of monks in their monasteries. The word "cell" later became the name for the units of which the organisms that make up all life are composed.

The magnification of Hooke's microscopes wasn't powerful enough to show the smallest life forms. A few years later an uneducated Dutch genius named Antonie van Leeuwenhoek, who lived from 1632 to 1723, was able to make microscopes that could magnify up to 300 times. He was such a perfectionist that he ground his own tiny lenses for his microscopes. With them Leeuwenhoek studied pond water, sand fleas, blood cells, all sorts of food particles scraped from between his teeth, and just about anything else he could get his hands on.

Antonie van Leeuwenhoek made his own microscopes with single lenses. They could magnify up to 300 times.

Here is Leeuwenhoek's description of what he saw in a drop of water: "I saw in it, to my great wonder, an incredible number of little animals of diverse kinds; some were 3 or 4 times as long as broad, but their thickness did, in my estimation, not much exceed that of the hair of a louse. They have a very pretty motion, often tumbling about and sideways."

Without knowing anything about them, Leeuwenhoek probably became the first person to actually observe those germs we call

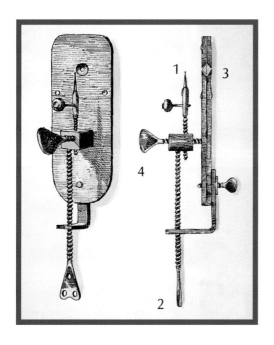

bacteria. The things his microscopes revealed astonished scientists of the time and helped set the stage for real advances in medicine. But progress was slow. Even after Leeuwenhoek's discoveries, it was another 250 years before anyone began to think about germs and how they influence our lives.

Leeuwenhoek made more than two hundred fifty microscopes like the one at left. With their aid, he was the first to describe and illustrate bacteria.

When microscopes became publicly available, people saw or imagined all kinds of little "critters" in their drinking water. This illustration called the water of England's Thames River "monster soup."

Three

Germs, Diseases, and Cells

How diseases spread remained a mystery for more than fifteen hundred years after the time of the ancient Greeks and Romans. Why one family member came down with a disease but another living in the same house avoided it couldn't be explained. In 1546 the Italian physician Hieronymus Fracastorius published a book on infection titled *Contagion*. In it he wrote: "Some persons are easily infected, others not," and "some persons can associate with the plague-stricken and take no hurt, others not." He also knew that some diseases affected only one part of the body, yet others spread rapidly and widely.

The Italian physician and philosopher Hieronymus Fracastorius (1483–1553) described germs and contagious diseases two hundred years before they could be detected under a microscope lens.

The Germ Theory of Disease

But Fracastorius added something new. Contagions, or diseases that could be caught, he said, are caused by germs, and "from the original germs other germs must be propagated that are similar . . . just as animals generate in their blood others like themselves."

When children get chicken pox or measles, they usually catch these diseases from their brothers and sisters, or from classmates. People realized a long time ago that many diseases are contagious and are passed on from one person to another. They are most likely to spread because, when sick people cough, they spray billions of germs into the air from their lungs or throat.

Today we call germs "microorganisms" because they are too small to be seen without a microscope. Every square inch of soil and many parts of our bodies contain billions of microorganisms, most of them bacteria. Bacteria were the earliest fully developed life forms on Earth and have been evolving into many thousands of different kinds for nearly 4 billion years.

Bacteria reproduce remarkably fast. In only twenty minutes one bacterium becomes two, then in another twenty minutes those two multiply and become four, and so on. At the end of a day or so, that one bacterium has produced billions more like itself. Bacteria live in the soil, deep underground in rocks, in all the waters of Earth, and in the air. They also live on the surfaces and insides of the bodies of all living things. Most are harmless, and we even need many of them to keep us alive. Bacteria living in the stomachs of cattle break down grass and hay into the sugars that nourish them. Without their bacteria, the cattle would die of starvation no matter how much they ate. We have

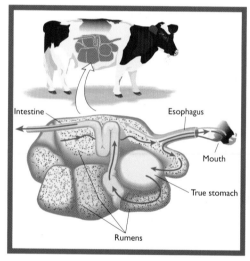

Intestine

Esophagus

Mouth

True stomach

Rumens

Cows and other ruminants have large extra sacs called rumens—the part of their digestive system where bacteria live. Although the cows cannot digest the grass they eat (light green arrow), these bacteria do the job for them by changing grass (dark green arrow) into nourishing sugars and proteins. The cow then provides us with milk and meat.

bacteria in our intestines that produce vitamin K, which helps clot our blood when we get a cut. Many bacteria produce still other vitamins and chemicals our bodies need.

Some bacterial germs are harmful. They are the ones that get into a cut or infect the intestines. We call these harmful germs *pathogens*. When there were fewer people in the world, there were fewer harmful bacteria, but as civilizations grew, germs multiplied right along with them. Large herds of animals also developed germs, some of which could be caught by people. Tuberculosis, for instance, was originally a disease of cattle, but it now infects many millions of people throughout the world. Bacterial infections of birds can cause serious pneumonia and other human diseases. Many other types of germs—*viruses* and parasites—are carried by mosquitoes and other insects.

Controlling Disease Germs

When disease germs get inside us, their growth must be controlled or they will overwhelm us and cause death. Over millions of years of evolution, living things have built very effective chemical defenses to combat germs. In a remarkable number of instances those defenses make us immune to many diseases. Ancient physicians knew this but did not understand how *immunity* worked. Nevertheless, some began to wonder if these defenses might somehow enable the body to resist various diseases.

One infectious disease that has been well known since ancient times is smallpox. Now known to be caused by a virus, the disease has caused millions of deaths and left people with hideous skin lumps and deeply scarred faces. In ancient times physicians observed that people who survived a mild case of smallpox never caught the disease again. Since that was so, some physicians reasoned, why not try to give a person a mild case of smallpox to prevent a worse infection? European physicians knew that other physicians in China, Africa, and India had long been doing just that. Eventually, in Europe around 1720, an English woman named Mary Wortley Montagu, whose face was badly scarred by smallpox, tried the method. She successfully infected her two children with a mild case of the disease and so made them immune. The method was called inoculation.

Inoculating someone involved collecting a small amount of pus from a person with a mild case of smallpox and then rubbing the pus into a freshly made scratch in the skin. With luck that person would then come down with only a mild case of the disease and so be immune for the rest of his or her life. It worked, and inoculation quickly spread through-

Smallpox was common in Africa and certain other parts of the world until 1976. Although it doesn't appear so, this child had only a mild case of the disease. Sometimes the entire face, arms, legs, and body became covered with running sores. When it was that bad, the patients usually died.

out Europe and America. But with smallpox there was no assurance that the inoculation would not kill the person rather than protect him or her from the disease. In fact, about 3 percent of people did die after receiving a smallpox inoculation. Doctors always worried about giving such a serious disease to children, and they wondered if there might be a safer way to protect against it. So common was the disease that "mothers counted their children only after they had had the smallpox."

Cows and Vaccines

In the late 1700s an English country doctor named Edward Jenner discovered a new method for inoculation. He was a mild-mannered man who wrote poetry and played the flute and violin. During his routine visits to treat patients living on farms in his area, he heard that the farm girls who milked cows never got smallpox. Why, he wondered? It turned out that these girls usually caught a disease called cowpox from the cattle they milked. Could deliberately infecting a person with cowpox make him or her immune to smallpox? Jenner concluded that it could. And since cowpox was only a mild and harmless disease, it seemed a much safer way to inoculate against smallpox than using the more dangerous live smallpox germs.

Jenner kept notes for twenty-five years before he finally worked up enough courage to try his first inoculation using cowpox germs. He inoculated a country boy named James Phipps. Jenner scratched the boy's arm and infected him with pus from a person with cowpox. After several anxious weeks, he tried to infect the boy with active smallpox. Nothing happened. Imagine his joy and relief when young Phipps did not become ill. Soon afterward the practice of vaccination—the word comes from the Latin word *vacca*, for "cow"—spread quickly throughout the world. Today, because of vaccination, the germs causing smallpox have all died, except for some germs still kept in laboratories. The last known case of smallpox anywhere was in India in 1977.

Until about 1830 few doctors believed in germs because germs couldn't be seen. That soon changed, however, when microscopes were made powerful enough to magnify things a thousand times larger than life. Many different kinds of bacteria could then be studied. While some scientists described various

Dr. Edward Jenner examining a milkmaid for cowpox sores. Those who came down with cowpox hardly ever caught smallpox. In the background a mother waits with her son to have him vaccinated.

kinds of bacteria they felt might cause illness, most doctors could not be convinced that germs caused disease. Many even said that they couldn't be bothered trying to use a microscope because it wouldn't tell them anything they didn't already know.

The Discovery of Living Cells

Hooke's "cells" took on new importance just before 1840, when increasing numbers of researchers studied bacterial and other living cells. Two German scientists, Matthias Schleiden and Theodor Schwann, discovered that animals are made up of millions and millions of cells that all seem to work together. Floating around within the sac wall, or membrane, were bits and pieces of strange looking structures. Most easily seen was a large central structure that they called the cell's *nucleus*.

In 1858 German scientist Rudolf Virchow reported on a study of cells of 23,000 specimens. He wrote the statement known today by every biologist: "All cells come from other similar cells." The French scientist Louis Pasteur found that bacteria do the same. This was the real beginning of modern medicine.

The famous German scientist Rudolf Virchow (1821–1902) realized that animals and plants are made up of different kinds of cells that all work together to maintain life. This caricature was drawn by the English artist Sir Leslie Ward.

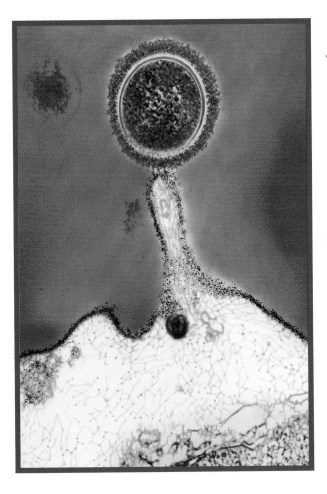

A large body cell (bottom) reaches out to capture a bacterium, which will be drawn into the cell for disposal.

Four

Wine, Hens, and Phagocytes

"Please save our chickens!" "Please save our wine!" "Please save our sheep!" These pleas came from French farmers and grape growers who were afraid of being ruined by enemies they couldn't see. Their pleas were directed toward the famous and beloved French chemist Louis Pasteur, who seemed to be able to work scientific miracles. Pasteur lived from 1822 to 1895.

Pasteur, the Miracle Worker

A chemist by training, Pasteur received an urgent message one day from the father of a classmate whose business was making alcohol from beet sugar. "The alcohol is no good," he said. Many French factories were having the same problem, and the country was losing millions of francs. Pasteur took samples of

The chemist Louis Pasteur (1822–1895) in his laboratory. He convinced doctors that bacteria cause illnesses, and he invented several vaccines to make people immune to infectious diseases.

beet mash from several vats and examined the mash under his microscope. It was infected with rod-shaped microorganisms that were feeding on the yeast cells, which were an important part of alcohol production. Most of the yeasts were shriveled and so were not reproducing. Pasteur told the industrialists to wash out the vats several times with boiling water and then put in fresh yeasts. That solved the problem and saved alcohol production throughout Europe.

Soon afterward Pasteur received the same request from French winemakers, who complained that their wines were bitter and spoiled. Again the vats were contaminated with bacteria that were destroying the yeasts. And again Pasteur advised cleaning the vats with boiling water. It worked and it saved the wine industry. At this time he also discovered how to prevent milk from going sour and beer from being spoiled. To solve these problems, he recommended mildly heating milk, wine, beer, and other

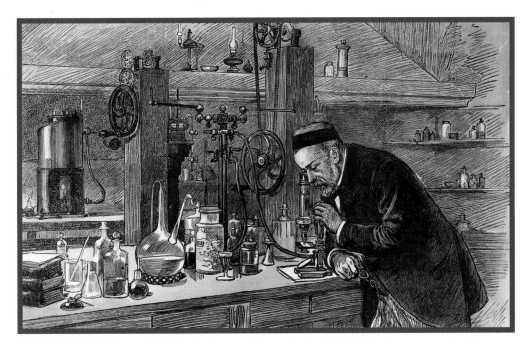

drinks to 144 degrees Fahrenheit (62°C). This heating process, which preserved them, is known today as *pasteurization*.

Pasteur next spent five long years finding a cure for a disease of silkworms, which saved the French silk industry. Then farmers begged him to find out what was causing sickness in their hens. Pasteur found that they were dying from a disease called chicken cholera. He discovered the tiny germs that were infecting the chickens and succeeded in growing colonies of the germs in glass containers so he could study them.

Pasteur knew about Jenner's use of weak cowpox germs to make people immune to smallpox. What if he could find a way to weaken the chicken cholera germs and then inject them into healthy chickens? Maybe that would give these chickens only a mild case of the disease, and after their recovery they might be immune to chicken cholera. After several months of experimenting, he found, almost by accident, that his laboratory colonies of germs could be permanently weakened just by leaving them alone for several weeks. When he injected healthy chickens with the weakened germs, they recovered. He next injected the recovered chickens with strong doses of the deadly germs. The hens just went about pecking as usual and showed no signs of coming down

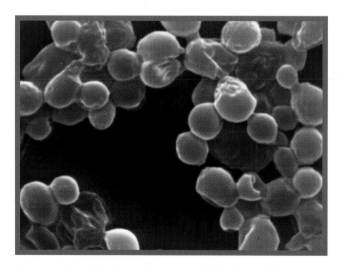

Pasteur started his investigations of infections by studying yeasts. In winemaking, these organisms produce alcohol and make wine during fermentation of the sugars contained in grapes. If the yeasts become infected, the resulting wine is sickening—toxic to taste.

Pasteur and his team vaccinate sheep in 1882. In this test, all of his vaccinated sheep lived, while those not vaccinated died after being exposed to virulent anthrax germs. This test finally proved the benefits of immunization.

with the disease. They had become immune. Pasteur called his preparation a *vaccine*, naming it after Jenner's cowpox vaccine.

When farmers heard that chickens could be saved by Pasteur's miracle methods, they asked him to study their sheep, which were dying all over Europe from a disease known as anthrax. Pasteur repeated what he had done to develop his vaccine against chicken cholera. He managed to weaken colonies of anthrax germs so that they could be used to make sheep and other animals immune to anthrax.

Many scientists doubted Pasteur's claims about the effectiveness of his vaccines. To prove his case, Pasteur asked all the doubters to witness an experiment. He injected his anthrax vaccine into twenty-four sheep, one goat, and several cows. He then isolated an equal number of animals that were not given the vaccine. A month or two later he injected all the animals in both groups with strong doses of *virulent*, or active and deadly, anthrax germs. All of his immunized animals remained healthy, but *every* one of the untreated animals died. The doubting scientists had to admit that Pasteur's claims were, indeed, sound.

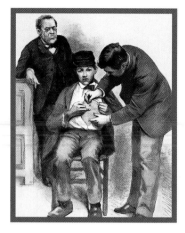

Another of Pasteur's achievements was his vaccine against rabies. In 1885, after many laboratory experiments, Pasteur looks on as a physician gives the first injection of his vaccine to Joseph Meister.

Before his life's work was finished, Pasteur managed to develop a vaccine for the dreaded disease called hydrophobia, or as it is more commonly called, rabies. This disease of mad dogs, wolves, raccoons, bats, and certain other animals is caused by invisible germs called *viruses*. Viruses can only reproduce in the living cells of other organisms. They are so unusual that some biologists even wonder if they are really living matter. A person bitten by an animal with rabies is infected with the rabies virus and without treatment is certain to die a horrible and painful death. When word spread that Pasteur had developed a vaccine for the disease, people flocked to Paris from all over Europe to be treated. In most cases they were saved.

Success and Tragedy

There could now be no doubt that germs cause disease, and that they get into the body in various ways. They can be swallowed in liquids, inhaled, or they may find their way into open wounds and cause infections. Around 1860 a young English surgeon named Joseph Lister suspected that many deaths after surgery were due to germs carried on the unwashed hands of attendants and surgeons and then transferred to patients during operations.

Joseph Lister was one of the first to understand the need to prevent bacterial infections in the operating room; his was equipped with carbolic acid spray to keep the air sterile.

Lister decided to wash and spray all wounds and his operating room with an antiseptic liquid called carbolic acid. He also required his assistants to wash their hands and surgical instruments with mercury chloride solutions. The results were astonishing. Imagine his delight when the rate of infection among his patients dropped to around 3 percent, while other surgeons had serious infection rates ranging from 50 to 85 percent.

The practice of cleanliness in hospitals did not take root as easily as Lister's success might suggest. At least one other attempt was tragic. In the late 1840s, a young Hungarian doctor named Ignaz Semmelweis was working on the childbirth ward at the University of Vienna Hospital in Austria. He suspected that infections contracted during childbirth on his ward were caused by medical students and birth attendants who failed to keep themselves and their clothes carefully washed, and by hospital workers who failed to keep the ward itself clean. Semmelweis noted that the rate of infections and deaths was much lower when women had their babies at home. He immediately cleaned up his ward by insisting that all medical personnel wash their hands with antiseptics before delivering babies. He also insisted on the use of clean bed linens instead of sheets previously contaminated by sick patients. Within two months, far fewer patients on his ward had infections after childbirth. Meanwhile, infections and deaths on the other wards remained as high as 10 to 25 percent.

The Hungarian physician Ignaz Semmelweis (1818–1865) was forced to resign his position at the University of Vienna because he criticized leading obstetricians for unknowingly infecting and therefore causing the deaths of many patients.

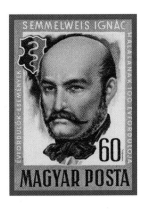

Instead of being praised for his work, Semmelweis was criticized and then fired. The professors of obstetrics resented being accused of killing their patients, though that is exactly what they were doing. Defeated, Semmelweis returned to his native Hungary, where he continued to speak out, accusing the great professors of not practicing safe medicine. But no one paid much attention to him, for he was not an accomplished speaker or writer. His frustration at being ignored while knowing that he was right grew and grew. Semmelweis eventually went mad and was committed to an insane asylum. Soon after, he died from infection with the same kind of germs he had been trying to fight.

From Bacteria to Bacteriology

The name for the scientific study of bacteria is *bacteriology*. The father of this branch of biology is the German country doctor Robert Koch, who lived from 1843 to 1910. Learning of Pasteur's work, he developed several ways to grow colonies of many different kinds of bacteria so he could study them more closely. One of Koch's associates, a chemist and physician named Paul Ehrlich, developed a way to treat the tragic disease called syphilis. It took Ehrlich 606 trials before he perfected his chemical treatment. It was an important accomplishment because it was a way of killing disease germs inside the body without doing great harm to the body's healthy cells.

Koch's associates also found cures for lockjaw and diphtheria. They developed a class of chemicals called *antiserums* that made the poisons produced by those disease germs harmless. But antiserums work only for a limited time because the body uses them up as they fight the bacterial poisons. This type of treatment was called *passive immunization* because the antiserums were not produced by the body itself. Later, vaccines were invented that made

Robert Koch (1843–1910) invented new ways to grow and separate different types of bacteria. He and Louis Pasteur are known as the fathers of bacteriology.

the body produce its own germ-fighting agents, so that type of treatment was called *active immunization*.

With the work of Pasteur, Koch, Ehrlich, and others, solutions to the puzzle of immunity were rapidly being found. One important piece of the puzzle was still missing, though: How did the body itself manage to kill germs? The puzzle master who provided the first answer to this question was a half mad but brilliant Russian scientist named Élie Metchnikoff. He did his major work in the 1880s. One day while studying the larval stage of starfish under his microscope, he became fascinated when he noticed small cells moving rapidly about inside the larvae. When he injected harmless, tiny particles of red dye into the transparent bodies of the starfish, these dye particles were soon gobbled up and disposed of. The cells also ate other foreign particles that Metchnikoff injected into the starfish larvae. Since he could see two types of these cells, he named the larger cells *macrophages*, meaning "big eaters," and the smaller ones *microphages*, or "little eaters." Collectively he called them *phagocytes*.

Phagocytes turned out to be nature's first line of defense against infections by germs. They simply ate up invading bacteria and other foreign agents. Humans and all other animals have these two kinds of cells in their blood and in various tissues throughout their bodies. Their discovery opened many new windows onto ways the immune system works.

Five

The Innate Immune System

Once he had discovered his "little eaters" and "big eaters" (microphages and macrophages), the Russian biologist Élie Metchnikoff wondered if these "garbage collector" cells might play a role in controlling infections by eating up germs.

Natural Immunity and How It Began

One day when he was observing small water fleas that lived in his garden pond, Metchnikoff saw one of the fleas swallow large yeast cells. Under his microscope he then saw that the yeasts

Élie Metchnikoff (1845–1916) was one of the founders of immunology. He discovered the white blood cells known as phagocytes, which eat up and digest invading bacteria. The phagocytes form the basis for innate immunity.

bored their way out of a flea's stomach and into its body. Almost at once, small, moving phagocyte cells attacked the yeasts and ate them up. But sometimes there were not enough phagocytes to control the yeast invasion. The yeasts then became so numerous that they killed the flea. Metchnikoff theorized that sometimes the yeast cells gave off a poison that drove the phagocytes back. However, most often the protective phagocyte cells of the body managed to kill the invaders. Here was part of the story of the body's control over infections. Today, we call it natural immunity. But how did the body's ability to protect itself start?

For more than 3 billion years in Earth's history, life forms were single-celled creatures that floated around in the warm seas, occasionally touching one another. Eventually they were

able to sense electrical or chemical changes on their surfaces when they were near other organisms. Cells that were exactly the same recognized one another as friends, but if they detected a foe, they quickly moved away or ejected poisonous chemicals that could drive those other cells away. Bacteria were the first to invent such "fight or flight" defenses, but all later organisms also came to have them.

Bacterial fossils that look very much like today's bacteria can be found in rock formations that are at least 3.5 billion years old. About 1.5 billion years ago, larger and more aggressive single-celled organisms called *protozoans* evolved. They include those curious creatures called amoebas and paramecia that you can easily see under a microscope. The early protozoans had a ready food supply—the limitless numbers of bacteria in the seas around them. The bacteria avoided becoming extinct by growing and reproducing very rapidly. Some evolved little "arms" or whiplike "legs" that enabled them to flee from danger more quickly.

Once in a while a bacterium consumed by a larger cell managed to remain alive inside it, becoming a part of the cell's machinery. What could be a safer home than living comfortably inside your enemy? One such early biological partnership is the green structure called a chloroplast found in plant cells. Others are the cell's powerhouse structures known as mitochondria. Bacteria that took up life inside larger cells in this way often shared their genes with the larger cell. Genes are those units of inheritance that determine your features, such as blue eyes, bushy eyebrows, or height.

About a billion years ago colonies of cells began to evolve. Today such primitive animals include sponges, jellyfish, and starfish. These many-celled, or *multicellular*, animals were at first made up of cells all of the same type, but later they began to accept different cell types into the colony. Among them were protozoans

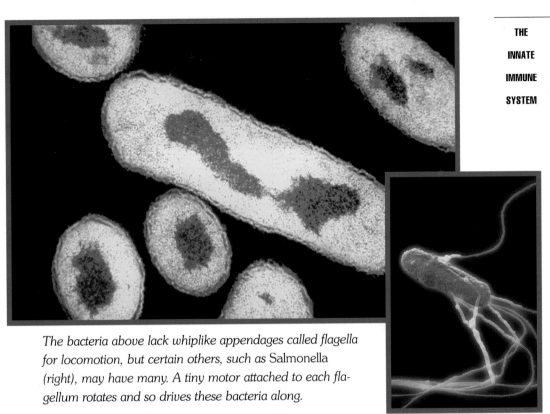

The bacteria above lack whiplike appendages called flagella for locomotion, but certain others, such as Salmonella (right), may have many. A tiny motor attached to each flagellum rotates and so drives these bacteria along.

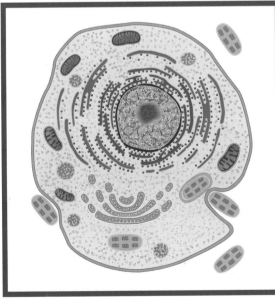

Long ago, free-living bacteria were captured by and became part of larger single-celled organisms. Plant cells are thought to have captured and incorporated chloroplasts (green bodies) in this way, as shown here in three stages. Mitochondria (purple bodies), the powerhouses of both plant and animal cells, most likely also were bacteria taken in by early cells in this way.

similar to Metchnikoff's phagocytes. They became specialized guardians of their colonies by providing protection—or immunity—from invading foreign agents.

Larger and more complex animals evolved over many millions of years. To survive, they needed ways to circulate food materials and assure that their guardian cells could move throughout their bodies. It wouldn't do to have deeper parts of the body open to attack by germs. Early primitive animals, such as sponges, sea worms, and squid, posted their guardian phagocyte killer cells throughout their bodies. These moved around in the circulating seawater that bathed their internal organs. But as

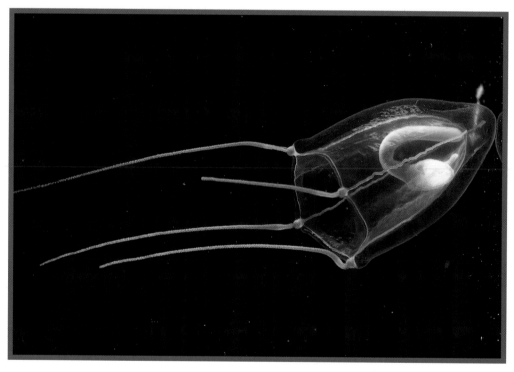

A box jellyfish 1¾ inches (4 cm) long. These animals are made up of ten to twenty different cell types, which may represent genetic contributions from various bacteria and other microorganisms the jellyfish has eaten.

organisms grew and evolved, even more efficient means of circulating these fluids were needed.

Evolution's answer to this problem was to develop tiny tubes to channel vital body fluids throughout the body cavities. These fluids carried energy supplies, protein-building materials, and cells of immunity to the farthest outposts of the body.

Still later in evolution, as oxygen became increasingly necessary, an iron-containing substance called *hemoglobin* developed. Hemoglobin molecules carried oxygen to all of the body's cells. Animals now had two systems of circulation to carry protective cells around: an open seawater circulatory system in simple animals and a closed system of blood vessels in more complex animals. In more complex animals certain vessels began to carry hemoglobin around the body.

Some six or seven million years ago a third kind of circulation developed. It consisted of lymphatic tubes that collect the clear body fluids that have bathed individual cells. This system developed only in those more advanced animals called *vertebrates,* which have backbones. Jellyfish and squid, which do not have backbones, are called *invertebrates.* Then the vertebrates developed a protective system of immune cells called *lymphocytes.* These began to circulate rapidly through the lymph vessels. Small structures called *lymph nodes* then appeared. They contain collections of different types of lymphocytes. We now know that only animals with backbones have evolved this much-improved type of immune system.

At first there were only a few lymphocytes, but over millions of years they evolved into several different types and their numbers greatly increased. Today, there are about one to two *trillion* lymphocytes in your body on guard to protect against foreign invaders.

All our blood cells and the cells of the immune system are produced in a soft substance that fills the cavities of our bones, called
bone marrow. The cells don't stay there very long but pass fairly
quickly into the blood and lymph vessels. Both kinds of cells develop from special *stem cells*, whose function is to develop into all the
different kinds of blood and lymph cells. Between 3 to 5 trillion
blood cells are formed in the bone marrow every day, but just

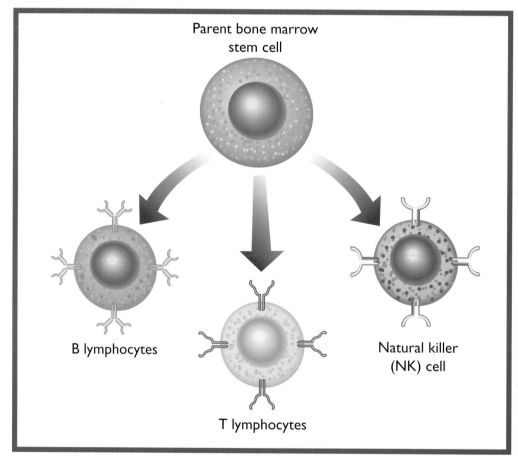

Parent bone marrow
stem cell

B lymphocytes

T lymphocytes

Natural killer
(NK) cell

*Stem cells in the bone marrow change into red blood cells, the phagocytes
of the innate immune system, and the different kinds of lymphocytes.
These lymph cells are carried by the blood to the lymph nodes and
thymus gland, where the new cells mature.*

about as many die, so their numbers are controlled. We are just now beginning to understand how stem cells change into red blood cells and the cells involved in immunity, and how they control the numbers of all the specialized cells into which they develop.

The two main types of blood cells are the red cells and the white cells. The red ones carry oxygen and nourishment to all the body cells. The white ones include the microphages and macrophages observed by Metchnikoff, as well as the lymphocytes of the immune system. Collectively the white blood cells are called leukocytes.

How Macrophages Do Their Work

By the 1890s researchers were routinely applying stains to cells so that they could study their many parts more closely. Today's powerful microscopes, which magnify things thousands of times, clearly show differences in blood cells and how they work. Electron microscopes can magnify up to one hundred thousand times a cell's actual size.

Once bacteria or any other foreign cells are eaten by phagocytes, they are drawn into a pool of strong chemicals, where they are dissolved and digested. If invading bacteria gain the upper hand and kill the microphage defenders, larger macrophage cells enter the battle to eat the bacteria and the damaged cells containing them. Fortunately for us nature has preserved our body cells' ability to wage chemical warfare by recognizing chemical differences between us and invading germs. These chemical systems first came to the attention of researchers in the late 1800s when they injected bacteria into the bloodstream of laboratory animals. The bacteria just disappeared from an animal's circulatory system and were never heard from again. How this happened was unknown then, but these defenses are now well understood.

The Complement Immune System

The chemical agents that make up the body's immune system are all proteins. These giant molecules are versatile. Not only do they provide nutrients and building blocks for a cell's many parts, but they also regulate the chemical activity of our cells and body tissues. For example, insulin is a protein that regulates the amount of sugar reaching our tissues through the blood. Another substance that is part of our immune system is called *complement*. It is made up of at least thirty different groups of proteins that are assembled in the liver. Complement continually circulates throughout the body in our blood and other fluids, ever on the lookout for germs and poisonous chemicals. Before going to work complement proteins first have to be activated by several other different chemicals. If they were active all the time, their powerful chemicals would rapidly dissolve all our regular cells, which would lead to death.

Complement protein molecules are activated and do their work in many carefully controlled steps. First, during infections, they sense the chemical poisons of invading germs and attach to them. Then they send out chemical signals to armies of microphages and macrophages to bring them to the scene of an infection. These activities usually stop the germs from rapidly reproducing, and most of them are killed. When that occurs, the infection is over, and the macrophages can begin to chew up and dissolve all the debris of dead bacteria and any body cells that were killed in the battle. If the invading bacteria were not controlled in this way, they would reproduce so fast that it wouldn't be long before there were more bacteria than normal cells in our bodies.

All of the reactions just described are part of the innate, or "built-in," immune system, which is called that because all its reac-

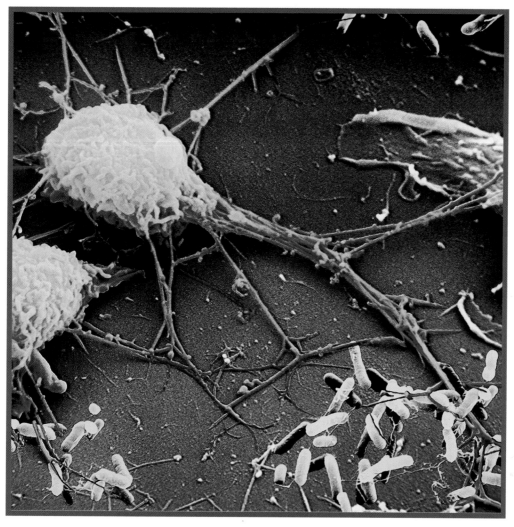

Macrophages (green-blue) reach out to capture live E. coli bacteria (yellow bodies) and the dead cell on the right.

tions are automatic. They don't need any previous experience to recognize and eliminate germs. More than 99 percent of infections are taken care of by the innate immune system. Nearly all of the remaining one percent are handled by a second and much more advanced immune system that evolved later.

Six

The Acquired Immune System

As animals evolved over many millions of years, they came to need an immune system that would work throughout the body. The system that evolved to do the job is called the *acquired immune system*. It is called acquired because it learns as it goes along. Its cells "remember" the threats to which the body has been exposed. For example, the acquired immune system is responsible for the immunity you get from vaccinations. Because its cells remember past infections, a second attack of a disease can be more quickly and effectively fought, as Pasteur and Jenner learned long ago.

Bone marrow cells, as enlarged more than two thousand times in this scanning electron microphotograph. Stem cells of the bone marrow develop into different kinds of cells. Among them are red blood cells (reddish disks) and white blood cells (round white objects). Bone marrow is a tissue that fills in the small spaces of spongy bone.

The lymphocytes of the acquired immune system are especially effective in stopping infections caused by viruses. They are much better at this than are the leukocytes of the innate immune system. One reason is that most of our one to two trillion lymphocytes move throughout the body day and night, searching for foreign invaders and cells infected by viruses.

Two Types of Lymphocytes

Our bone marrow produces two different types of lymphocytes. One type, called *B-lymphocytes*, or simply B-cells, are produced at the rate of about one billion a day. After B-cells mature and begin to function in the bone marrow, they move into the lymph node

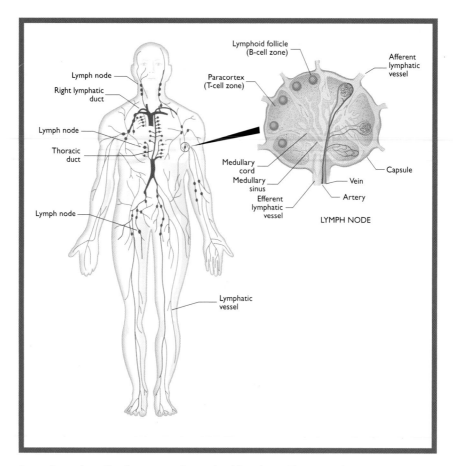

Lymph, a clear fluid, escapes from the blood capillaries and nourishes all cells of the body. The lymph carries sugars and proteins to all of the body's cells. It also carries waste materials back to the blood for disposal through a large lymph vessel called the thoracic duct.

storage areas, where they refine their activities. They are kept ready to reproduce whenever they are needed. In little more than a week one lymphocyte can produce twenty thousand new B-cells whenever an infection occurs. About ten thousand lymphocytes pass through an average lymph node every second, and there are hundreds of lymph nodes, so many new B-lymphocytes can be developed. Although B-cells don't attack or eat germs, they produce chemical antibody substances that can kill or disable them. Those substances coat and disable bacteria or other germs so that white blood cell macrophages come to the rescue and kill the invaders. Macrophages are very effective and will attack almost anything. Bacteria, a wood splinter, foreign chemicals, or anything else that should not be in body tissues are all taken in by macrophages and digested.

Although antibody chemicals don't actually kill germs, they can cure diseases such as diphtheria and tetanus by making the poisons of the disease germs harmless. Antibodies

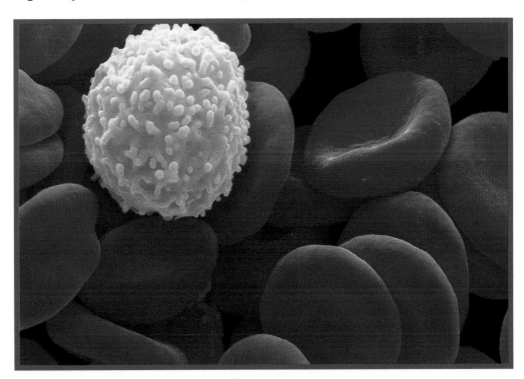

Disk-shaped red blood cells outnumber white blood cells. The red cells carry oxygen to all of your other body cells. The white cells, microphages, fight invading germs. Both cell types develop from stem cells in the bone marrow. This scanning electron micrograph magnifies the cells 3,500 times.

also clump bacteria together so they can be more easily eaten by phagocyte cells. They can stop most viruses from infecting healthy cells of the body. All of these activities stand ready to back up the innate immune system when needed.

The second type of lymphocytes are *T-lymphocytes*, or T-cells. They learn how to recognize foreign invaders during their stay in the thymus gland, which is located in the upper part of the chest. About a trillion T-cells develop in the body. B-cells have only short lives, but more and more of them can be made on demand. T-cells, however, are made to survive during a person's entire lifetime. But as a person ages and the T-cells begin to die, they are not replaced. After about age thirty-five, the immune system gets less and less effective because of these losses.

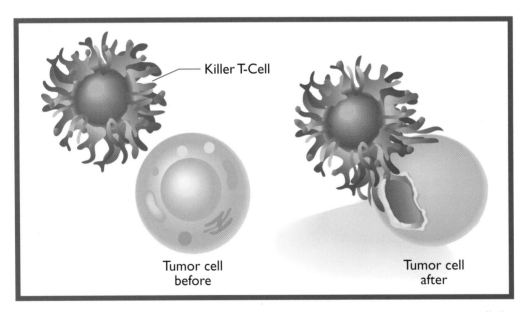

Killer T-Cell

Tumor cell
before

Tumor cell
after

Killer T-cells get rid of damaged cells or dangerous cancerous tumor cells by first attaching themselves to these unwanted cells. Then they drill a hole in the target cell's surface to kill the cell. Sometimes they inject strong poisons into the target cell as well.

T-cells are organizers rather than doers. *Helper T-lympho-cytes* examine foreign invaders and then sound the alarm, if needed. Macrophages, B-lymphocytes, and other immune cells are then attracted to the battle. Helper T-cells also instruct other killer cells to do away with cells that have been infected with viruses. The killer cells drill holes in infected cells and inject powerful chemicals to kill them.

Why don't the chemicals and cells of the immune system attack and kill normal cells of the body? How do they know us from the enemy? This is a question that has only recently been answered. By the time they are mature our immune cells have been trained to ignore our own normal chemicals and cells. Before they can "graduate" from the bone marrow and thymus gland, lymphocytes must be able to tell the difference between our own cells and foreign agents. If they can't they are killed off at once. Surprisingly only 3 percent of T-cells pass the test. Day and night the cells of our immune system sample all our tissues to see if they are healthy.

How the Body Fights Infection

Your body resists infection in several ways. The first line of defense is the skin, which is a barrier to germs. Whenever the skin is pricked or cut, bacteria enter through the opening. Bacteria are everywhere, and billions are just waiting for a chance to enter a wound. Over millions of years of evolution, however, people have developed many different ways to fight invasions of bacteria and viruses.

When you cut your finger, you bleed. Blood vessels near the wound swell open a bit and enable a free flow of the blood bacteria and antibodies, which immediately coat the surfaces of the invading bacteria. The blood also carries millions of those

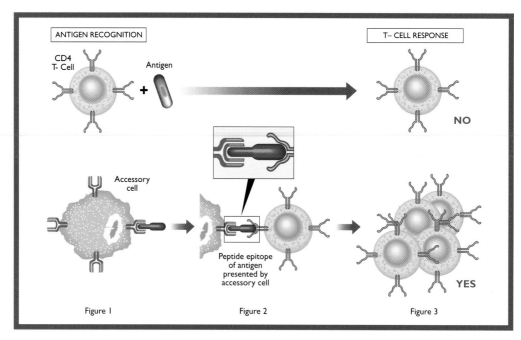

T-cells cannot be activated by foreign chemical antigens alone (top) to kill the harmful antigen. The antigen first has to be broken down by an accessory cell, such as a macrophage (1, bottom). Then this simpler protein is taken into the T-cell (2). This causes the T-cell to stimulate the formation of a much larger number of now activated T-cells (3), which are tailor-made to deal with that particular antigen.

"little eaters" called microphages. Attracted to the bacteria by the antibody coating, the microphages quickly begin to engulf and digest the bacteria. In most cases the struggle is soon over, the bleeding stops, and the wound heals. It becomes a little red because the skin has been irritated by the bacteria and by the chemicals used by the microphages to digest them.

Occasionally the invading bacteria may produce poisons that overwhelm and kill the microphages. In that case the dead microphages become food for the bacteria rather than the other way around. When that happens, the bacteria keep multiplying by dividing into two new organisms every twenty minutes. At the end of six hours, if not controlled, each bacterium would be able to produce more than half a million new ones. If the bacteria gain the upper hand and an infection gets out of control, serious chemical poisonings can occur. People have been known to die from a small thorn prick when they were unfortunate enough to be infected with particularly nasty bacteria.

S everal of our body organs and tissues produce and use different cells of the immune system. BLOOD, for example, is a tissue that carries white blood cells (leukocytes) and lymphocytes to places where they are needed. LYMPH, also a tissue, is a clear fluid that carries the lymphocytes around the body. It also carries dead and damaged bacteria to the lymph nodes for disposal.

Important Parts of the Immune System

Your LIVER is an organ that makes complement proteins. Complement can also serve normal cells by regulating their chemical activity in many different ways. The SPLEEN is another important organ of immunity. It acts like a huge lymph node and produces large numbers of lymphocytes as soon as an infection signals the need for them. The spleen also rounds up stray bacteria that have escaped from other parts of the immune system, and it destroys red blood cells when they get old. The walnut-sized THYMUS GLAND is also an extremely important immune organ that serves as a training school for all the lymphocytes that are destined to become T-cells.

Whenever the body's immune system wins the battle, there are many dead and dying cells at the site of the infection. Then, the "big eater" macrophages are attracted to the scene and begin to clean up by eating and dissolving the dead foreign matter. After this has been done the blood vessels shrink to their normal size and function, and the episode is over.

With each such infection we get, the cells of our immune system remember the chemical poisons of the invading bacteria. The

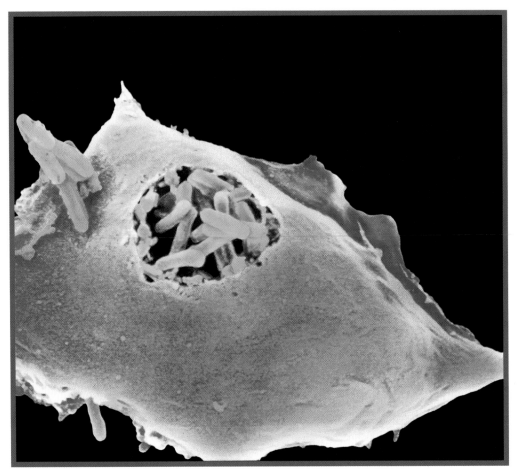

Sometimes, bacteria (green bodies) kill the phagocytes (large orange object).

result is that the next time the same kinds of bacteria invade the body, our immune system knows just how to fight them off. It also responds much faster the second time. This *secondary immunity* is part of the acquired immune system and is the kind of immunity we receive through vaccinations.

Does the Immune System Ever Fail?

Defects in the immune system are rare, but they do occur. When things go wrong, we can develop ailments such as arthritis, thyroid inflammation, multiple sclerosis, and other disorders. Or if the antibacterial defenses are missing, we can get one infection after another.

Sometimes a child is born without a thymus gland, which means that the immune system cannot develop T-cells. The child is then very likely to get infections. Other parts of the immune system can be damaged or become inactive. Occasionally a person is born with all the immune functions missing. Unless such people are protected with medicines and isolated from infections, they will die at a young age. One such child, the famous "bubble boy," lived in a plastic tent with filtered air for twelve years. He finally died from a viral infection when doctors tried to introduce genes that he lacked into his body, hoping that this would provide him with an immune system.

The immune system sometimes get out of control. It may begin to attack the body's normal cells. This is most likely to occur if bacterial poisons attach to certain types of body cells. Heart valve cells or parts of our joints are commonly affected. In such cases inflammations attack the heart valves or cause arthritis in the joints. Since all of our body systems are regulated by genes, certain people with abnormal genes are more likely to get such diseases than are others.

Seven

Immunity Today

Before vaccinations against disease became common, at least 50 percent of the children born in Europe and the United States died from infections. Today, government medical scientists recommend inoculation against eleven common diseases to which we may be exposed during our lifetime. Because the immune systems of older people weaken with age, it is important for those over age sixty-five to be vaccinated against flu and pneumonia.

Effects of Vaccinations

Modern vaccines injected into your arm during a vaccination are made in several ways. One uses live but weakened disease germs that enable your immune system to recognize the disease and fight it later, if necessary. Another uses certain pro-

After vaccination, lymphocytes and other white blood cells develop fingerlike projections that fasten onto infecting germs, which are then attacked and destroyed by other cells of the immune system.

tein vaccines made in the laboratory. Both ways enlarge the immune system's "memory banks" and prompt the killing of germs that cause infection. Children who are not vaccinated are twenty times more likely to catch common diseases, such as measles, than children who have been vaccinated. Even so, some groups of people protest against vaccination because of their religious or other beliefs. They say that vaccinations can cause serious illnesses, or even death. Although such results

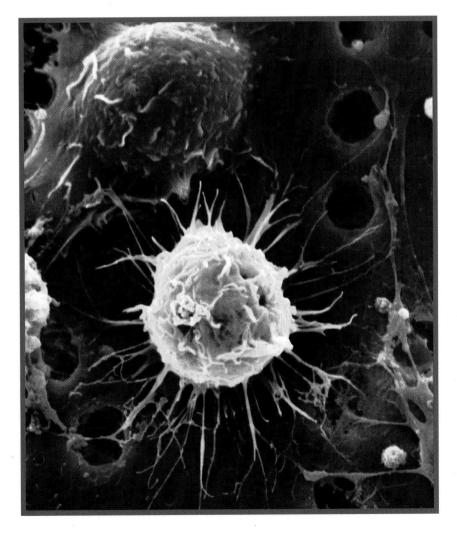

do occur, they are extremely rare. For every child harmed by vaccination, more than one hundred thousand are saved from life-threatening infections and death. It should be recognized, however, that some medical authorities feel it is sometimes better for children to be exposed to common childhood diseases in the belief that their immune systems will be stronger as a result of acquiring, and recovering from, those diseases on their own.

AIDS

AIDS stands for "Acquired Immune Deficiency Syndrome." It is caused by infection with a virus known as HIV, which stands for "Human Immunodeficiency Virus." The virus enters the body in

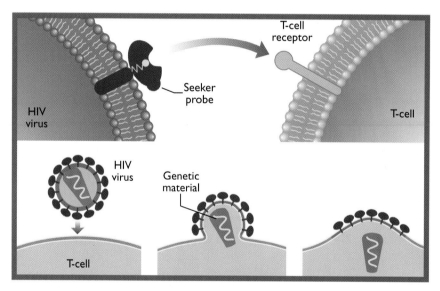

How viruses enter and infect healthy body cells: An HIV (AIDS) virus first attaches itself to a T-cell. Notice that the seeker probe of the virus must exactly match the T-cell's receptor probe. Once the virus is attached, it injects its genetic material into the T-cell. This causes the infected cell to produce huge numbers of HIV viruses, which escape and go on to infect and kill more T-cells.

fluids during certain sexual acts and in dirty needles exchanged by drug addicts. It then seeks out and kills T-cells, the very cells that are supposed to prevent infections. It takes several years for a person infected with HIV to lose enough T-cells to become seriously ill. Then they come down with fevers, a cough that won't go away, painful swollen gums, intestinal problems, and severe

Overactive Immune Systems

An overactive immune system can be just as dangerous as an underactive one. Asthma and allergies such as hay fever may develop when we inhale pollens, molds, or other proteins carried in the air. Certain cells in the throat and lungs then react by producing a powerful chemical called histamine, which causes sneezing and clogs our noses and sinuses with mucus. Histamine also causes small blood vessels to swell. We may take an *anti-histamine* to ease our discomfort. Antihistamine drugs are also given to people with asthma, a condition that occurs when mucus and narrowing of our breathing tubes make breathing difficult.

When a heart, kidney, or other organ is transplanted, it often sets off a chemical alarm that tells the immune system that foreign cells have entered the body. Killer T-cells then attack and try to destroy the new heart, kidney, or other transplanted cells that contain the "wrong" kind of protein. The solution to this problem is to turn off the overactive immune system with medication so that the newly transplanted organ is no longer rejected.

weight loss. Eventually, every organ in the body is affected, including the brain.

First discovered in Africa around 1977, AIDS is now spreading rapidly throughout the world. Today at least 50 million people carry the HIV virus; 2.3 million people died of AIDS in just one year, 1997. More than 500,000 have died of the disease in the United States since 1980, and there is no sign of any decrease in the number of new cases. In some African countries more than 60 percent of the population now has AIDS. Although not everyone with the HIV virus comes down with AIDS, most do. Scientists are working hard to develop vaccines against AIDS, but so far without success because the viruses are well hidden in infected cells, and the immune machinery needed to kill them is no longer active enough.

Other virus-caused diseases have also appeared since the late 1970s. One, called Ebola, has struck western Africa. It causes high fever, internal bleeding, brain damage, and rapid death. To date, there is no known way to treat people infected with the disease. The virus is carried by monkeys, chimpanzees, and humans. One African family contracted the disease when the children found a dead chimpanzee. They brought it home, their mother cooked it, and everyone ate it. So far Ebola has not gotten out of Africa, although a related strain was brought into the United States from the Philippines in a laboratory monkey. Many scientists believe that it will be only a matter of time before the Ebola virus spreads around the world.

Still other new viral infections will continue to appear just as they have for millions of years. The West Nile virus, which is carried by mosquitoes and related to yellow fever, and two deadly viruses found in the western United States are other new disease organisms that are causing great concern. Right now no vaccines are being produced to fight any of these viruses.

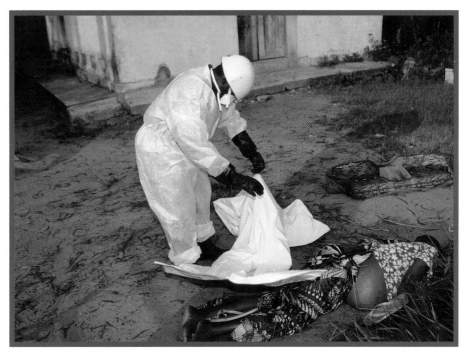

A woman in Kikwit, Zaire, Africa, died of Ebola virus infection only one day after she began to feel sick. Ebola is deadly, and there is no known defense against it, or cure.

Antibiotics and Their Abuse

In the 1940s the wonder drug penicillin was developed, with the hope that it would overcome all infectious diseases. Since then many more antibiotics have been produced, but we are still far from stopping bacterial diseases. In fact, bacteria keep developing ways to render antibiotics ineffective almost as rapidly as new antibiotics are created in the laboratory.

From 1980 to 1992, despite all the antibiotics available, deaths from diseases caused by infections rose 58 percent, and ear infections in children skyrocketed 67 percent. Today, many bacteria resist nearly all antibiotics, and deaths from infections in hospital patients are increasing. The bacteria are able to resist

Like people, dogs, and salamanders, bacteria have those units of inheritance called genes. Also like other organisms, the activities of genes can change through mutation by being exposed to radiation or to harmful chemicals or, as happens in bacteria, through an exchange of genes.

How Germs Fight Antibiotics

Suppose that a lot of germs get into a cut and cause a bad infection. A doctor gives the patient an antibiotic that goes to work and kills off the bacteria faster than they can reproduce. Suppose also that one bacterium in one thousand has exchanged genes with another bacterium and, as a result, has become resistant to the antibiotic. In this case it survives and produces millions more just like itself—all resistant to the antibiotic.

In every population of bacteria there are a few exceptional ones like the altered bacteria just described. For just about any antibiotic we humans can make in the laboratory there will be one or more mutant bacteria able to resist it. And that is why it may prove to be dangerous in the long run to use any of those so-called "antibacterial" cleansers, soaps, and other such products available on our supermarket shelves.

Overuse of antibiotics is bad because bacteria can rapidly adapt to almost any new chemical attack against them. Not only may antibiotics not do any good, but in many cases they can do harm by killing off good bacteria that help keep the dangerous ones under control. When the number of beneficial bacteria is lowered too much, dangerous germs, including bacteria, yeasts, and protozoa, are likely to multiply rapidly and take over.

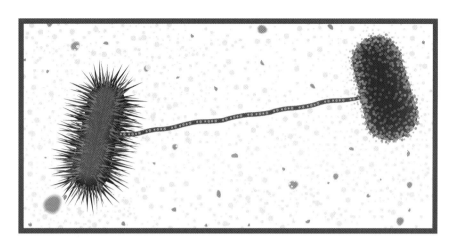

Bacteria exchange genetic material first by linking together through a string-like probe. The probe then contracts and draws the two bacteria to touch side-by-side. Genetic material is then exchanged between the two.

antibiotics by exchanging genetic materials with one another and with different kinds of germs that are resistant to antibiotics. These genetic changes are often caused by an overuse of antibiotics and by antibacterial soaps that claim to kill "99.9 percent of germs," but this claim can be misleading. A number of bacteria thrive on soap, and even in bleach. Because bacteria reproduce so rapidly, many new resistant germs can crop up almost overnight. Also, people who demand antibiotics for practically every ailment, and doctors who prescribe them unnecessarily, are often responsible for creating bacterial resistance to antibiotics.

Many medical scientists think that a large number of dangerous types of bacteria actually have been produced by the overuse of antibiotics. Tuberculosis is an infection that was once almost eliminated by antibiotics, but the genetic material of the tuberculosis germs now enables them to resist almost all antibiotics. As a result, the disease is again on the rise in the United States, with 500,000 new cases during 1999 alone. Worldwide, at least 2 million people die from tuberculosis each year.

The meat industry has helped bring about some of the worst effects of the overuse of antibiotics. For many years cattle have been fed an antibiotic called tetracycline to make them grow larger and fatter. Over the years genetic materials have changed the bacteria living in the cattles' intestines. Although harmless to the cattle, these bacteria, among them *E. coli* 0157, are dangerous for humans, especially young children. Several times a year there are outbreaks of illness from eating hamburgers and other meats served by fast-food outlets. This dangerous *E. coli* strain causes inflammation of the intestine, bleeding, shock, and in some cases death.

For several years chickens have been fed the antibiotic Cipro to fatten them for sale. Cipro was once effective in fighting serious infections, but because of its widespread use it is rapidly becoming ineffective for many intestinal diseases. Not only is this valuable antibiotic becoming less effective, but its use in patients may even be harmful because it delays proper diagnosis and treatment of sick people.

The recent demand for Cipro to prevent people from catching anthrax, which is being spread by terrorists, is bound to have the same effect. The problem of antibiotic resistance is already very serious in hospitalized patients. Most antibiotics used to treat postoperative and hospital-acquired infections with *Staphylococcus aureus* and enterobacteria are now almost completely ineffective because these germs are so common in hospitals and have so often been exposed to many different antibiotics.

What's in the Future?

Is it possible that bacteria, viruses, and other disease agents may eventually endanger human existence as the world's population continues to climb? Many medical scientists now believe that our human immune systems are weakening because of pollution, the overuse of antibiotics, and exposure to those "smart" germs. Whether or not raging epidemics may eventually destroy all human life is now being debated.

Throughout history there have been many severe epidemic diseases, such as outbreaks of the Black Death during the Middle Ages; the worldwide influenza epidemic of 1918–1919; and now AIDS, along with other deadly diseases, such as Ebola and the West Nile virus. In addition to all the naturally occurring disease agents out there, more are hidden away in the military laboratories of Russia, the United States, Iraq, and other countries. It is not impossible that one day these disease agents could fall into the hands of terrorists. Of all crimes against humanity, biological warfare may be the most ghastly.

But to suppose that any attack by bacteria, viruses, or protozoa—natural or intentionally perpetrated by people—could wipe out the entire human population is unrealistic. Although millions of people have died during past epidemics, never more than 30 to 40 percent of the many populations infected with an epidemic disease have been wiped out. Humans and other animals have been around long enough to evolve immune systems capable of fighting off even the most harmful disease agents. Like "smart" bacteria, our human populations are genetically "smart" enough to resist any germs nature may throw our way. And the healthiest among us are the ones who will survive and pass our effective immune systems along to the next generation. As our ability to replace bad or weak genes with good or stronger ones through genetic engineering rapidly increases, so does our ability to keep the battalions of disease germs at bay and under control.

Glossary

Acquired immune system—that part of the immune system that learns as it goes along by remembering the germs and foreign proteins to which the body has been exposed; it also is responsible for the immunity you get from vaccinations.

Active immunization—immunity produced by deliberate exposure to *antigens*, such as weakened or killed germs.

Antigen—substances, usually proteins, that produce immune responses in living organisms, and that then react with the antibodies or T-cells of the immune system.

Antiserums—proteins produced by B-cells that react against germ products or other antigens. They can be separated from the blood serum for medical uses.

B-lymphocytes—small oval cells made in the bone marrow that are kept in the lymph nodes, the spleen, or in the circulatory system. Also called B-cells, B-lymphocytes multiply in large numbers when they sense an infection or foreign antigen, and they produce antiserum that is specific to that one antigen.

Bacteriology—the scientific study of bacteria and related single-celled organisms.

Bone marrow—the soft fatty material that fills the bone cavities and makes blood cells.

Complement—bacteria-killing proteins produced by the liver.

Helper T-lymphocytes—"carriers" that transmit proteins and other antigens to the surfaces of B-cells and T-cells, signaling them to attack foreign cells.

Hemoglobin—a red oxygen-carrying pigment found in red blood cells.

Immune system—the combination of cells, organs, and proteins that protect the body against invasion by bacteria and other foreign cells and substances.

Immunity—protection against a specific threat; in medicine, the body's ability to fight off infection by microorganisms.

Invertebrates—animals without backbones, such as squid, jellyfish, and sea worms.

Lymphatic system—small thin-walled vessels that return fluids to the bloodstream and nourish the body tissues. It also plays a major role in the immune system through actions promoted by the lymph nodes.

Lymph nodes—clusters of lymphocytes through which the body's free-traveling lymphocytes pass at a rate of more than ten thousand lymphocytes per lymph node per second.

Lymphocytes—small cells of the immune system that develop from stem cells into B-cells or T-cells.

Macrophages—the "big eater" phagocytes.

Malaise—feeling ill.

Microorganisms—tiny living things that can be seen only under a microscope. They may be of animal or plant origin.

Microphages—the "little eater" phagocytes.

Multicellular—animals or plants composed of many cells that may be of one kind or, usually, of different kinds.

Nucleus—the relatively large structure that acts as the control center for the cell.

Passive immunization—immunity against disease agents that have already invaded our bodies. The immunizing agents are serums made in the laboratory.

Pasteurization—heating milk or other liquids to destroy harmful microorganisms. It can be done by keeping a liquid at 144 degrees Fahrenheit (62 °C) for thirty minutes or at 176 degrees Fahrenheit (80 °C) for fifteen to thirty seconds without affecting its flavor.

Pathogens—disease-producing microorganisms.

Phagocytes—cells that surround and eat other cells and organisms such as bacteria or microscopic parasites, and foreign bodies such as splinters.

Plague—widespread and highly contagious bacterial disease carried by rats and their fleas.

Protozoans—the simplest organisms in the animal kingdom. Single-celled and containing cell nuclei, they can vary in size from microscopic to macroscopic (seen with the naked eye).

Secondary immunity—immunity that, once established, can strengthen and rapidly deal with infective disease agents or other toxic products that the body has already experienced.

Stem cells—unspecialized embryonic and adult cells that can develop into all tissues of the body. Also cells of the bone marrow that develop into red blood cells and all the cells of the immune system.

Symptoms—headache, pain, or other such bodily changes associated with illness.

T-lymphocytes—those lymphocytes that mature in the thymus gland after being produced in the bone marrow.

Vaccine—a collection of killed or weakened germs, or of their antigenic proteins, given to people or animals to provide immunity.

Vertebrates—animals with backbones, such as people, sharks, and salamanders.

Virulent—highly contagious or damaging, especially used to describe pathogens.

Viruses—infectious microscopic agents too small to be seen with ordinary light microscopes. They can reproduce only by invading a living cell and borrowing the infected cell's metabolic machinery.

AIDS—a rapidly spreading viral disease that progressively destroys the immune system, making people vulnerable to many infectious diseases.

Anthrax—a disease of cattle and sheep that can be transmitted to humans. The germ, *Bacillus anthracis*, causes spreading sores on the skin. It also can be inhaled and can cause severe pneumonia. It can cause death by infecting all tissues of the body, including the bloodstream and the brain. Some nations are cultivating anthrax for use in bacterial warfare.

Black Death—infection by the bacillus *Yersinia pestis* carried by rats and their fleas. Those afflicted suffer from high fevers, terrible weakness, black hemorrhages in their skin, severe coughing, and early death. The disease can also be transmitted from patient to patient by coughing.

Chicken pox—a very contagious but mild childhood viral disease. It causes itching, sores, and scabbing on the face and abdominal skin. In adults it can cause nerve damage and severe pain even to those who have had childhood chicken pox.

Cowpox—a mild skin disease of the hands and wrists caused by contact with cowpox lesions on the udders of milking cows. It leaves no scars. It was the original source of the vaccine against smallpox.

Diphtheria—a common childhood infection that used to kill about half of all children born. It is caused by a bacterium that makes a poison, mostly in the throat. The throat cells thicken and produce a tough membrane over the breathing tubes. But it is the poison that usually kills by weakening the heart and the nervous system. Antiserums are highly successful against the disease.

E. coli 0157 infection—a strain of the E. coli bacillus found in meats that can cause severe infection in the intestines, especially of children. It is not part of the E. coli flora that normally live in the intestines.

Epilepsy—recurrent seizures with shaking fits, unconsciousness, and disturbances of the vision. The seizures are caused by abnormal electrical discharges in the brain.

Flu—short for influenza, it is caused by viruses. It is usually mild, with headache, a sore throat, and coughing, but some strains are severe and lead to death.

Hydrophobia—a virus whose name means "fear of water," it is also called rabies. People bitten by an animal carrying the rabies virus develop painful muscle spasms, particularly in their throats, and they can no longer swallow. The disease may take up to several months to develop, depending on how far away the bite is from the spinal nerves or brain. Once established in the nervous system, it is always fatal.

Leprosy—a slow, progressive disease that causes scaling and lumps in the skin, nerve damage, thickening of the bones of the face, and loss of the fingers and toes. The bacterium causing the disease is somewhat similar to the one that can cause tuberculosis.

Lockjaw—is caused by the germ Clostridium tetani, which usually enters the body through a puncture wound and makes a nerve poison as it grows. This poison causes spasm of all the muscles of the body, but especially of the jaw muscles, which pull the teeth together so a person can't swallow. Sometimes the person can't breathe and suffocates. An antiserum can help in the early stages of the disease.

Measles—a very infectious viral disease that causes a runny nose, red eyes, sensitivity to light, a hacking cough, and small red spots all over the body. The lymph glands become very swollen. It occasionally causes brain fever and death. Also called rubeola.

Pneumonia—inflammation of the lung tissues caused by many kinds of bacteria and viruses. The small air sacs become filled with swellings and fluid collections, impairing oxygen intake.

Smallpox—the virus causing smallpox no longer exists, except in military medical laboratories, where it is being preserved for possible use in biological warfare. Smallpox causes high fevers and chills, severe headaches, muscle pain, and enlarging skin rashes that ooze and bleed. In the past it was highly lethal, and severe scarring occurred in those who survived.

Syphilis—a disease transmitted through sexual activity that causes sores and swelling of the lymph glands. Skin rashes appear from six to twelve weeks after the swelling. The rashes then clear up and the patient can appear to be healthy for a number of years, but the germs continue to spread internally. Eventually they affect the brain, large blood vessels, and bones.

Tuberculosis—an infectious disease that mainly affects the lungs and bones. The germs are slow-growing and destructive. Lung hemorrhages are common, but the heart, brain, and other organs can also be affected. There are several types of the mycobacteria germs that cause the disease.

West Nile virus—a potentially deadly affliction carried by mosquitoes that have bitten infected birds. It causes viral brain infections (encephalitis) in old people and others with reduced immune defenses.

Whooping cough—severe coughing spells with the medical name pertussis. A vaccine made of pure proteins is now used to prevent reaction to the disease germs.

Further Reading

Brandon, C. G. F., ed. *Ancient Empires*. New York: Newsweek Books, 1973.

Cartright, Frederick F., and Michael D. Biddis. *Disease and History*. New York: Sutton, 2000.

Clendenning, L. *Source Book in Medical History*. New York: Dover Publications, 1942.

Cooper, G. M. *The Cell*. Washington, D.C.: ASM Press, 1997.

"Defeating Aids: What Will It Take?" *Scientific American* (Special Report), pp. 81–107, July 1998.

Dobell, C. *Antony van Leeuwenhoek and his "Little Animals."* New York: Dover Publications, 1978.

Dubos, R. and P. Maya. *Health and Disease*. New York: Time Life Books, 1974.

Fracastorius, Heironymus. *Contagion, Contagious Diseases, and Their Treatment*. Translated by C. W. Wright. New York: The Knickerbocker Press, 1930.

Gerhart, John, and Marc W. Kirschner. *Cells, Embryos, and Evolution*. Malden, MA: Blackwell Sciences, 1997.

Hooke, Robert. *Micrographia* (1665). Reprint, New York: Dover Publications, 1961.

Kipple, K. F., ed. *Plagues, Pox, and Pestilence*. New York: Barnes and Noble Books, 1997.

Kolata, Gina. *Flu: The Story of the Great Pandemic of 1918*. New York: Touchstone Press, 1999.

Lane, I. W., and Susan Baxter. *Immune Power*. New York: Avery Publishing, 1999.

Lappe, Marc. *The Tao of Immunity*. New York: Plenum Press, 1997.

Sompayrac, Lauren. *How the Immune System Works*. Malden, MA: Blackwell Sciences, 1990.

Trachtman, Paul. "Hero for Our Time: Louis Pasteur and Anthrax," *Smithsonian*, pp. 34–41, January 2002.

Wrench, G. T. *Lord Lister: His Life and Work*. New York: Frederick Stokes, 1920.

Page numbers for illustrations are in **boldface**.

AIDS (Acquired Immune
      Deficiency
      Syndrome), 62–64,
      62, 69
allergies, 63
amoebas. *See* protozoans
ancient Egyptians, 6–8,
      10
ancient Greeks, 8, 10, 12,
      24
anthrax, 35, 68
antibodies, 53
antibiotics, 65–68
      Cipro, 68
      overuse, 66–69
      penicillin, 65
      tetracycline, 68
antiserums, 38
asthma, 63

Babylonians, 8
bacteria, 23, **23**, 26–27,
      30–31, **31**, 33,
      38–39, 42, **43**, 47,
      48, **49**, 53-59, **58**,
      65–67, **67**, 69
      E. coli 0157, 68
      See also germs
bacteriology, 38
biological warfare, 69
Black Death. *See* plague
blood, 9, 27, 46, 48, 55,
      57
bone marrow, 46, 51, 55
"bubble boy," 59
Bushmen, 7

carbolic acid, 37
cells, 22, 30–31, **31**, 33,
      36, 38-39, 40–42,

43, 44–49, 50–55,
      51, **53**, 57, 59,
      63–64
chicken cholera, 34–35
chicken pox, 26
chloroplast, 42, **43**
circulatory system
      closed, 45
      lymphatic, 45
      open, 45
complement, 48, 57
Contagion, 24
cowpox, 29, 34–35
crisis, 15

Dioscorides, 20
drugs (medicines), 7, 11,
      13, 14, 21, 59, 63

Ehrlich, Paul, 38-39
Empedocles, 12–14
epilepsy, 11
evolution, 41–45, 49, 50,
      55, 69

flu. *See* influenza
Fracastorius, Hieronymus,
      24, **25**, 26

genes, 42, 59, 66
germs, 13, 17–18, 20–23,
      25–27, 29–30,
      34–36, 38–39, 40,
      44, 47–49, 53, 55,
      60–61, 67, 69. *See
      also* bacteria;
      pathogens; viruses
gods, 8, 10, 11, 13, 15, 21
      Asclepius, 8
      Hygeia, 8

Ishtar, 8
Shamash, **9**
Sin, 9

Hammurabi, **9**
heart, 9, 63
hemoglobin, 45
Hippocrates, 10–12, 14–15
histamine, 63
Hooke, Robert, 22
Human Immunodeficiency
      Virus. *See* viruses,
      HIV
humors, 11, **12**, 14

illness (disease)
      ancient ideas about, 6,
            8, 11, 14–15, 21
      effect on animals, 6,
            27, 34–36
      effect on humans, 6,
            27
      spread of, 17-20,
            24–26, 36
      symptoms, 14
      ways body fights, 15,
            27, 39, 41, 45, 47,
            48–49, 53, 55–59,
            69
immune system, 15, 20,
      39, 45–47, 48–49,
      54–55, 57–58,
      60–63, 69
      acquired, 50–51
      failure, 59
      innate, 48–49, 51, 54
immunity, 27–29, 34–35,
      39, 41, 44–45, 47,
      50, 57

secondary, 59
immunization
    active, 39
    passive, 38
infections, 21, 37–38,
    40–41, 48–51, 55,
    57–66, 68
influenza, 18–19, 60, 69
inoculation, 28–29, 60
insulin. *See* proteins
invertebrates, 45

Jenner, Edward, 29, **30**,
    34, 50

Koch, Robert, 38–39, **39**

Leeuwenhoek, Antonie
    van, 22–23, **22**
leprosy, 19, **20**
leukocytes (white blood
    cells), 47, 51, **51**,
    53, **53**, 57
Lister, Joseph, 36–37, 37
liver, 57
lymph, 57
lymph nodes, 45, 51–52,
    57
lymphocytes, 45, **46**, 47,
    51-52, 57, **61**
    B-lymphocytes (B-cells),
        51–54, 55
    T-lymphocytes (T-cells),
        54–55, **54**, **56**, 57,
        59, **62**, 63

malaria, 13
measles, 26, 61
medicine men, 7, **8**
Meister, Joseph, **36**
mercury chloride, 37
Metchnikoff, Élie, 39,
    40–41, 44, 47

Micrographia, 22
microorganisms, 33
microscopes, 21–23, **21**,
    23, 26, 30, 33, 39,
    40, 42, 47
mitochondria, 42, **43**
myths, 7–8

nucleus, 31

operations, 9, **14**

Paracelsus, Phillipus
    Bombastus
    Aurelius, **15**
paramecia. *See*
    protozoans
pasteurization, 34
Pasteur, Louis, 31–36,
    32, **35**, **36**,
    38–39, 50
pathogens, 27
phagocytes, 39, 41, **41**,
    44, **46**, 47, **49**,
    54, **58**
    macrophages, 39, 40,
        47, 48, **49**, 53, 55,
        58
    microphages, 39, 40,
        47, 48, 56
Phipps, James, 29
physicians, ancient, 6, 7,
    9–10, **11**, **13**, 14,
    19–21, 27
plague (Black Death),
    16–18, 69
plants, medicinal, 7,
    10–11, 20–21
pneumonia, 27, 60
priests, 7–8
proteins, 48, 57, 61, 63
protozoans, 42, 66, 69

rabies (hydrophobia), 36
Ramses III, **7**

Schleiden, Matthias, 30
Schwann, Theodor, 30
Semmelweis, Ignaz,
    37–38, **37**
shamans, 7, **8**
skin, 55
smallpox, 18, 27–30, **28**,
    34
spleen, 57
stem cells, 46, **46**, 47
superstitions, 10
syphilis, 38

Thucydides, 18, 20
thymus gland, 54–55,
    57, 59
tuberculosis, 27, 67

vaccination, 29–30, 50,
    59, 60–62
    effects, 60–62
vaccine, 35–36, 38, 60,
    64
Varro, 21
vertebrates, 45
Virchow, Rudolf, 31, **31**
viruses, 27, 36, 51,
    54–55, 68
    Ebola, 64, **65**, 69
    HIV, 62–64, **62**
    West Nile, 64, 69

witch doctors, 7–8, **9**,
    10, 20

yeasts, 33, **34**, 40–41, 66

William L. Donnellan is a surgeon and historian of science.
After serving in the Royal Canadian Air Force and the U.S.
Navy, he obtained his bachelor of arts degree in chemistry and
zoology at the University of Texas, and his M.D. at McGill
University in Montreal, Canada. He completed residencies in
general and children's surgery at hospitals in Boston, Ann Arbor,
Michigan, and Chicago. He served on the staff at Children's
Memorial Hospital in Chicago for many years. In 1981, he
earned his Ph.D. in the history of science at Northwestern
University. Dr. Donnellan has served as a Traveling Fellow,
studying surgery and pathology in Vienna and Switzerland from
1959 to 1960. He has lived and worked in many other countries, among them South Africa, Saudi Arabia, Hungary, and
Holland. He is the author of numerous scientific publications
and of a major textbook of surgery, *The Abdominal Surgery of
Infancy and Childhood*, which was published in1996. During the
course of his life, Dr. Donnellan has been a downhill ski racer, an
accomplished violinist, a professional photographer, and a flight
instructor, with 2,500 hours of flying time. He and his wife,
Laura, live and work in Rangeley, Maine.